Cloudy

By Alice K. Flanagan

Look up at the clouds in the sky. What sizes and shapes do you see?

Small, white clouds dot the sky above this field.

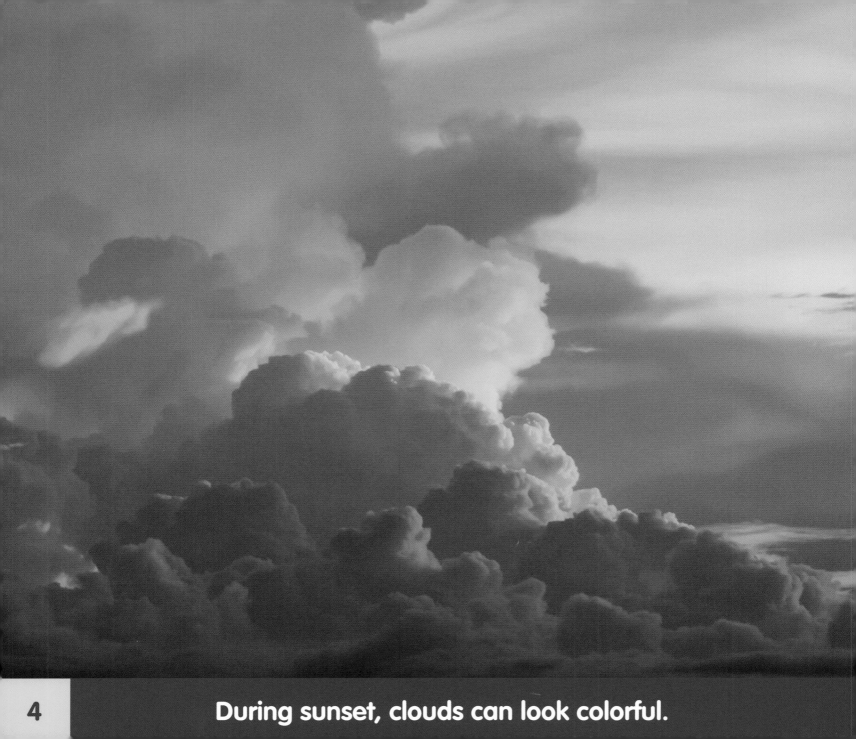

During sunset, clouds can look colorful.

There are several types of clouds. Each type has its own shape. Some types of clouds are higher in the sky than others.

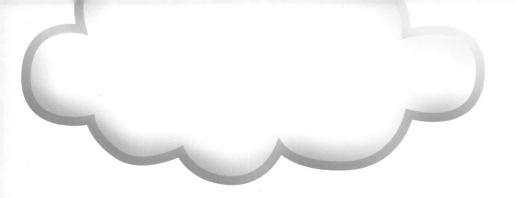

Some clouds look like big mountains in the sky. These clouds can bring rain. They can also bring thunder and lightning.

The tallest and biggest clouds can bring thunder and lightning.

Thin clouds sometimes look like feathers.

Some clouds look like feathers or horses' tails. These clouds are usually high up in the sky.

Other clouds cover the sky
like blankets or ocean waves.
They have curly tops and
make lots of neat shapes.

The tops of clouds can be seen from an airplane.

These clouds are forming over the Atlantic ocean.

What are clouds? Clouds are tiny drops of water in the air that have joined together.

Sometimes the drops become too heavy to stay in the air. Then they fall as rain. If the air is cold enough, the drops fall as snow.

Rain from these clouds is falling over a forest.

Storm clouds can get very dark.

Not all clouds bring wet weather. White, feathery clouds usually do not bring rain or snow. Dark clouds usually do bring rain or snow.

Clouds can bring dangerous weather, too. They can bring **tornadoes** and **hail**. Sometimes this weather causes **damage**.

A dangerous tornado comes down from a cloud.

Many types of clouds can dot the sky.

Look up at the sky. Can you tell what type of weather the clouds will bring today?

Glossary

damage (DAM-ij): Damage happens if something is harmed. Hail can cause damage to a car.

hail (HAYL): Hail is made up of tiny balls of ice that fall from the sky. When hail falls, you can see it on the ground.

tornadoes (tor-NAY-dohs): Tornadoes are swirling tubes of air that come down from the sky. Some clouds can bring tornadoes.

To Find Out More

Books

Delano, Marfe Ferguson. *Clouds*. Washington, DC: National Geographic Kids, 2015.

DePaola, Tomie. *The Cloud Book*. New York, NY: Holiday House, 2011.

Jensen, Belinda. *A Party for Clouds: Thunderstorms*. Minneapolis, MN: Millbrook Press, 2016.

Websites

Visit our website for links about clouds:
childsworld.com/links

Note to Parents, Teachers, and Librarians: We routinely verify our Web links to make sure they are safe and active sites. So encourage your readers to check them out!

Index

About the Author

Alice K. Flanagan lives with her husband in Chicago, Illinois, and writes books for children and teachers. Today, she has more than 70 books published on a wide variety of topics, from U.S. presidents to the weather.

The Child's World®
childsworld.com

Published by The Child's World®
1980 Lookout Drive • Mankato, MN 56003-1705
800-599-READ • www.childsworld.com

Photo credits: Artorn Thongtukit/Shutterstock.com: 11; Dan Ross/Shutterstock.com: 19; Jeff Gammons StormVisuals/Shutterstock.com: 7; kavram/Shutterstock.com: 16; majeczka/Shutterstock.com: 3; Pakhnyushchy/Shutterstock.com: 12; rbrechko/Shutterstock.com: 8; sbw18/Shutterstock.com: 15; Sunny Forest/Shutterstock.com: 20; urbans/Shutterstock.com: cover, 1; Worachat Limleartworakit/Shutterstock.com: 4

ISBN Hardcover: 9781503827868
ISBN Paperback: 9781622434541
LCCN: 2018939780

Printed in the United States of America • PA02398